POCKET IMAGES

Black Country
Aviation

The Black Country Society

This voluntary society, affiliated to the Civic Trust, was founded in 1967 as a reaction to the trend of the late 1950s and early 1960s to amalgamate everything into large units and in the Midlands to sweep away the area's industrial heritage in the process.

The general aim of the Society is to create interest in the past, present and future of the Black Country, and early on it campaigned for the establishment of an industrial museum. In 1975 the Black Country Museum was started by Dudley Borough Council on 26 acres of totally derelict land adjoining the grounds of Dudley Castle. This has developed into an award-winning museum which attracts over 250,000 visitors annually.

There are over two thousand members of the Black Country Society and all receive the quarterly magazine *The Blackcountryman*, of which over 105 issues have been published since its founding in 1967. In the whole collection there are some 1,500 authoritative articles on all aspects of the Black Country by historians, teachers, researchers, students, subject experts and ordinary folk with an extraordinary story to tell. The whole constitutes a unique resource about the area and is a mine of information for students and researchers who frequently refer to it. Many schools and libraries are subscribers. Three thousand copies of the magazine are printed each quarter. It is non-commercial, and contributors do not receive payment for their articles.

PO Box 71 • Kingswinford • West Midlands DY6 9YN

First published 1994
This new pocket edition 2007
Images unchanged from first edition

Nonsuch Publishing
Cirencester Road, Chalford
Stroud, Gloucestershire, GL6 8PE
www.nonsuch-publishing.com

Nonsuch Publishing is an imprint of NPI Media Group

British Library Cataloguing in Publication Data.
A catalogue record for this book is available from the British Library.

ISBN 978-1-84588-407-9

Typesetting and origination by NPI Media Group
Printed in Great Britain

Contents

The mighty propeller of the Wolverhampton-built Boulton Paul Sea Balliol in the Aerospace Museum at Cosford, dwarfing little Joey Brew (also Wolverhampton-built). One of the finest aircraft museums in the world, Cosford sits on the edge of the Black Country, inspiring new generations in the wonderful world of aviation.

Introduction

Apart from police and air ambulance helicopters flying overhead, aviation is hard to find in the Black Country these days. A trip to the annual air display at RAF Cosford, or its marvellous Aerospace Museum, is the nearest most Black Countrymen come to an aircraft, but it was not always so.

Probably the most historic aviation event in the Black Country took place as long as ago as 1862, when a balloon taking off from the Stafford Road Gas Works in Wolverhampton set a new World Altitude Record, with a flight higher than Everest.

One of the earliest airfields in Great Britain was created at Dunstall Park in Wolverhampton in 1910, and was inaugurated with the first All-British Flying Meeting, in June of that year. Much later municipal airports were built at Walsall and Wolverhampton, and the Black Country even had its 'own' airline for a while, Don Everall Aviation. During the Second World War an RAF airfield was built at Perton, right on the edge of the Black Country, near to a First World War satellite landing ground.

All these airfields have gone now, often without trace, but it is in manufacturing that the Black Country has most connection with the world of aviation. As the main metal-bashing area of the country there has hardly been a British aircraft built without Black Country-made parts in it, but the region has had two major aircraft manufacturers of its own.

In 1913 the Sunbeam Car Company decided to enter the 'sunrise' industry of aviation and began to build aero-engines. At the beginning of the First World War it was the only major aero-engine manufacturer in Great Britain, and built thousands of its water-cooled engines, particularly for the Royal Naval Air Service. It also built several hundred aircraft of Short and Avro design.

In 1934 the aircraft department of Boulton & Paul of Norwich was sold off and became Boulton Paul Aircraft Ltd. It sought a site for a new factory, and Wolverhampton offered the best package, next to its new municipal airport at Pendeford. Moving to Wolverhampton in 1936 the company built 2,198 complete aircraft at the new factory, as well as parts for countless others, including the powered flying controls for which it is now famous. Its most celebrated product was the Defiant fighter, which fought in the Battle of Britain alongside the Spitfire and Hurricane, and was the most successful British night fighter during the Blitz.

Boulton Paul became Dowty Aerospace Wolverhampton but the famous name and initials of the company are maintained by the Boulton Paul Association, made up of ex-employees and others anxious to preserve the history of Black Country aviation, and Boulton Paul Aircraft in particular. Current projects include the restoration of two Boulton Paul Balliol front fuselages, and the collecting of Defiant parts to create the most complete example outside the one in the RAF Museum, Hendon.

Staffordshire and Black Country Aviation history is perpetuated by the Staffordshire Aircraft Restoration Team, who own and restore around twenty aircraft and aircraft cockpits. Some are on display at Abotts Bromley and Wolverhampton, others are in store, awaiting the day when thy can all be gathered together at a suitable venue.

One

Before the First World War

The coal-gas-filled balloon *Mammoth* about to take off from Stafford Road Gas Works, Wolverhampton, on 18 August 1862, its second flight from the site. On 5 September, on its third flight, it broke the World Altitude Record, with a height in excess of 30,000 ft.

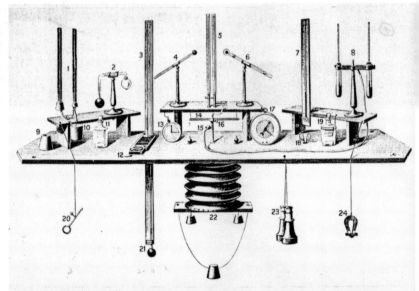

THE INSTRUMENTS PREPARED BY GLAISHER for use during high-altitude balloon ascents. They are 1, dry and wet bulb thermometers; 2, Daniell's hygrometer; 3, mercury barometer; 4, blackened bulb thermometer for exposure to the sun's rays; 5, wet and dry bulb thermometers connected with aspirator; 6, similar to No. 4, but contained in a vacuum tube; 7, sensitive thermometer; 8, Regnault's hygrometer connected with aspirator; 9, one of the shields used to keep sun off wet and dry bulb thermometer; 10, water container for wet bulb; 11, bottle of water; 12, compass; 13, chronometer; 14, minimum thermometer; 15 and 16, taps to control aspirator; 17, aneroid barometer; 18, scissors for cutting string; 19, ether for Daniell's and Regnault's hygrometers; 20, magnifying glass to read instruments; 21, weight to keep barometer vertical; 22, foot-operated aspirator; 23, binoculars; 24, magnet for moving compass needle.

There were many balloon ascents in the Black Country, mostly of a less scientific nature than that of the *Mammoth*. This one is ascending from the Molineux football ground on 25 May 1901, showing that the use of balloons for advertising is anything but a new phenomenon.

Opposite above: James Glaisher (left), the scientist who initiated the flights of the *Mammoth* to make scientific observations at high altitude. On the third flight he passed out from lack of oxygen. Henry Coxwell (right), an eminent aeronaut who built and flew the *Mammoth*.

Opposite below: The scientific instruments which Glaisher took aloft.

In 1902 the Wild West showman Samuel Cody flew the man-lifting kite he was experimenting with from West Park, Wolverhampton, while his show 'Klondyke Nugget' was in town. This photograph shows him operating the winch, but on the South Downs, the following year.

This is an example of Cody's man-lifting kite, an invention he sold to the War Office. He is standing at the wing-tip, also on the Downs in 1903.

Stanley Spencer's 40,000 cu. ft airship en route from the Corbett Hospital Fête at Ambelcote to Brierley Hill in August 1905. It was hired as an attraction instead of the balloon which was a usual feature of the fête.

Spencer's workshop in Highbury, North London, showing the framework of the airship's car being assembled in 1903. This was the first practical airship built in this country.

The first all British flying meeting took place at Dunstall Park, Wolverhampton from 27 June to 2 July 1910.

The Hartill monoplane, built by Edgar Hartill, a Wolverhampton plumber, to the order of a Dr Hands, for the first All-British Flying Meeting, held at Dunstall Park in June 1910. It failed to fly.

Captain George William Patrick Dawes' Humber monoplane after he stalled and crashed on 17 June. After repairs he was able to demonstrate the necessary skills to obtain his Aviator's Certificate (No. 17) on 26 July, also at Dunstall Park.

The engine shop of Star Engineering, Frederick Street, Wolverhampton in 1910. The engine in the foreground is believed to be their first 40 hp aero-engine.

The Star monoplane at Dunstall Park in 1910. Designed, like its engine, by Granville Bradshaw, it failed to fly in this form, and took no part in the meeting.

Opposite above: Officials standing by one of the six hangars erected along the canal-side of Dunstall Park, no doubt discussing the appalling weather which dogged the meeting.

Opposite *below*: Claude Grahame-White, one of the most famous aviators of the day, flying his Farman biplane, with Oxley sidings in the background.

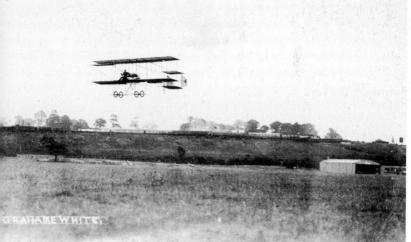

GRAHAME WHITE.

Dolly Shepherd, a famous parachutist of the day, about to ascend at Dunstall Park during the 1910 meeting. The basket of the gas balloon which will lift her aloft is hidden by the crowd of men; her parachute lies on the ground. Apart from the trapeze bar in her hands, her only other means of support is a sling between her legs.

Right: A minute later she is being carried aloft, her parachute suspended under the basket. She is holding the bar with one hand and waving to the crowd with her other! At an appropriate altitude the parachute was released, and she floated to the ground.

Below: A postcard on sale during the meeting. A certain amount of artistic licence has been used, as the heavily laden monoplane is flying over West Park, not Dunstall Park!

Graham Gilmour flying his Bleriot monoplane near the 'control tower' which had been erected in the centre of the course. He had recently become the first Scotsman to fly in Scotland, and was to die in a flying accident in 1912.

Another view of Claude Grahame-White in the air. He was to win the prize money for the greatest aggregate flying time at the meeting.

The Avis monoplane of H.J.D. Astley. This was designed and built by the Dudley-born brothers Howard and Warwick Wright, in their Battersea workshops.

HON C.S. ROLLS ON CROSSCHANNEL MACHINE

The Wright biplane of the Hon. Charles Rolls, who had founded a car company with an engineer named Henry Royce not long before. In this aircraft he had recently made the first double crossing of the Channel. At the next flying meeting, two weeks later at Bournemouth, it broke up in the air and killed him.

Above: Ernest Willows' airship *City of Cardiff*, which he based at Dunstall Park for a while in 1911. It is pictured at Cranford on 17 May, where he alighted for breakfast at the home of Mr A.L. Dennison on a flight from Wolverhampton to Leamington.

Opposite below: An aerial photograph taken from Willows' airship by Captain G.M. Maitland in 1911. It shows Autherley Junction, Pendeford, looking little different than it does today.

Right: Willows returned to Dunstall Park in 1912 to operate this gas-filled balloon. It is about to make its first flight, 85 miles to Aberystwyth.

Below: Aerial views of Wolverhampton taken a few minutes later. On the left are the grandstands of Dunstall Park, with the railway viaduct very prominent, and on the right West Park is evident.

Above and below: This is the 18,000 cu. ft balloon *Bee* being inflated at the Knowles Oxygen Company, Wolverhampton in April 1912. Hydrogen was more expensive than coal-gas, but could lift more. *Bee* made a flight to Bridgnorth and then Abergavenny, in company with the coal-gas balloon *Meteor*.

Opposite: Balloon ascents from Dudley Castle were regular attractions; G.P. Lampriere alone made thirty-nine ascents from there. This one is by Stanley Spencer in 1912.

The redesigned and rebuilt Star monoplane at Dunstall Park in 1911, showing its Star engine. This engine is now on display in the RAF Museum, Hendon.

The redesigned Star monoplane at Dunstall Park, where it is believed to have made one flight in the hands of Joseph Lisle. A contemporary report also states that Granville Bradshaw flew it at Dunstall Park and Brooklands.

Right and below: Gustav Hamel, who won the 1913 air race over a circular course from Birmingham (which included a landing at Walsall), shown here in a Bleriot monoplane at the Central Athletic Ground, Chadsmoor, Cannock, also in 1913.

Gustav Hamel in his Bleriot monoplane at Stafford in 1913. He was one of the most famous aviators of the day, and gave demonstration flights all over the country. He disappeared over the Channel in 1914.

Walter Davies of Dudley in the first of two gliders he designed and built. He first flew this one on 27 May 1911 at Dudley. The other first flew in 1913 at Halesowen.

Two

Sunbeam Aero-Engines

Jack Alcock, the pilot engaged in 1913 by the Sunbeam Car Co. of Wolverhampton to test their first 150 hp aero-engine in the Farman biplane which is shown behind him. In 1919 with Arthur Whitten-Brown he became the first man to fly the Atlantic non-stop, flying a Vickers Vimy.

Left: Sunbeam's second aero-engine, the V12, 225 hp side-valve Mohawk. This was the most powerful British aero-engine available at the start of the First World War.

Below: Sunbeam's extraordinary 475 hp Viking, with three rows of six cylinders and twin overhead camshafts. Though intended for aircraft, its 1,400 lb weight largely restricted it to motor boats.

Opposite above: The Sunbeam bomber, serial N516, the sole Sunbeam-designed aircraft to be built powered by their own Arab engine. It was not a success, but Sunbeam built 646 aircraft designed by other companies.

Opposite below: The 200 hp V12 Sunbeam Arab, one of the worst disasters of the First World War. Ordered in huge numbers almost off the drawing board, it was never made to work properly.

Left: The first double crossing of the Atlantic was by the airship R34, powered by Sunbeam engines.

Below: The Sunbeam Maori engine as fitted to the R34.

One of 541 Avro 504s built by Sunbeam, mostly with rotary engines. This one is fitted with their own excellent 100 hp Dyak engine, and is at Dunstall Park, showing that flying took place there after the First World War.

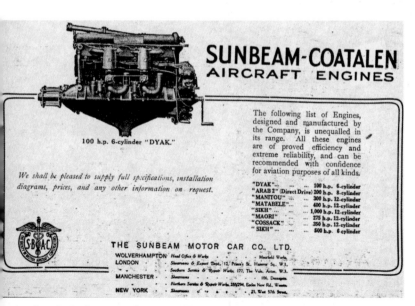

An advert for Sunbeam aircraft engines, 1921.

Airship gondolas, complete with 350 hp Sunbeam Cossack engines, in production at the Sunbeam factory. They might be for the R36, R37 or R38.

A gondola for the R37 ready for delivery. Post-war airship work petered out, and in fact the R37 never flew. Sunbeam soon withdrew from aviation altogether.

Three

First World War Manufacturing

RE7s being built in 1915 by Austin Motors at Longbridge. This was not in the Black Country of course, but it shows J.D. North (the tall man in the dark suit on the right) who was superintendent of production despite being only 23 years old. In 1917 he joined Boulton & Paul in Norwich, and became Managing Director and then Chairman of Boulton Paul Aircraft in Wolverhampton from 1936 until his death in 1968. He was one of the great aviation pioneers.

Handley Page 0/400, J2258, one of 104 built by the Birmingham Carriage Company at Smethwick, and flown from a field at Halford's Lane. They also built 100 DH10 medium bombers.

ABC Dragonfly engines in production at Clyno Cars, Pelham Street, Wolverhampton. This photograph shows practically their entire production from the 500 ordered, after cancellations at the end of the war.

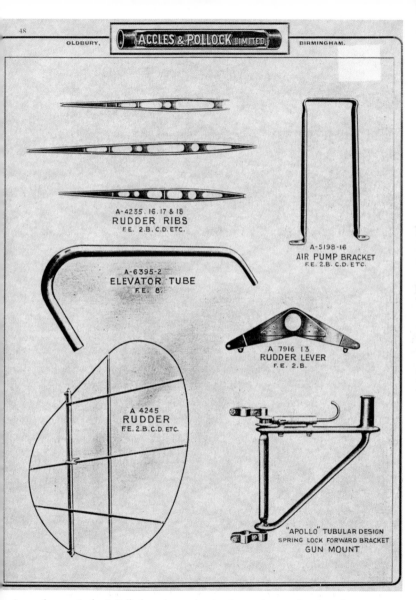

A-4235. 16. 17 & 18
RUDDER RIBS
F.E. 2.B. C.D. ETC.

A-5198-16
AIR PUMP BRACKET
F.E. 2.B. C.D. ETC.

A-6395-2
ELEVATOR TUBE
F.E. 8.

A 7916 13
RUDDER LEVER
F.E. 2.B.

A 4245
RUDDER
F.E. 2.B. C.D. ETC.

"APOLLO" TUBULAR DESIGN
SPRING LOCK FORWARD BRACKET
GUN MOUNT

A page from an Accles & Pollock catalogue, showing they made more than just tubes.

Guy Motors
LIMITED

Manufacturers of
Aero Engines &
Commercial Vehicles.

BRITISH Design, Materials
& Workmanship.

MERITS — Efficiency,
Economy & Durability.

Guy Motors Ltd.,
Fallings Park,
Wolverhampton.

Guy Motors of Wolverhampton built ABC Wasp and Dragonfly engines, but are known to have delivered only one of each before cancellations at the end of the war.

Four

Walsall Airport

Avro 504K, G-EBKR, of Berkshire Aviation Tours, giving joy-flights at Calderfields, Walsall in the late 1920s. They were one of the most famous of the barnstormers, who brought aviation to so many people in the 1920s and 1930s.

Another view of G-EBKR at Calderfields, which was the usual venue for the barnstormers, including Alan Cobham's Flying Circus during the mid-1930s.

An Avro 504N, G-ACOK, in the mid-1930s, with a ladder placed alongside for passengers to climb aboard. This aircraft had been built by Sunbeam but was refitted with an Armstrong-Siddeley Lynx radial instead of the old rotary.

Aircraft gathered for the official opening of Walsall Airport on the Aldridge Road, 6 July 1935.

A Kirby Kite glider being flown by Amy Johnson at Walsall Airport on 2 July 1938. On her third landing she turned it over, but was not badly hurt.

John Carter and Bill Holmes in the Walsall Aero Club's Miles Hawk at the airport.

The Westland Widgeon, G-EBRO, owned by Ivor Tidman, and a resident at the airfield in the late 1930s.

Above: The Utility Airways DH Fox Moth, G-ACEY, which crashed while giving joy-flights at a South Staffs Aero Club garden party on 24 September 1938. The pilot took off uphill with a full load on a hot day, realized he would never be able to climb, and deliberately stalled into the trees to prevent a worse accident!

Opposite below: A most unusual visitor to Walsall on 23 April 1936 was this Vought Corsair flown by Flt. Lt. Edwin Shipley (now Group Captain), a club member on a flight home from Martlesham Heath, where it was being evaluated.

Right: A young apprentice engineer, Eric Holden, leaning on the strut of Ivor Tidman's Widgeon. He later became Manager of Wolverhampton Airport.

Below: South Staffs Aero Club members in front of the hangar. Left to right: Ivor Tidman, -?-, Dick Haynes, Eileen Jones, 'Chink' Haynes, ? Weston, Norman Jones, Mrs Jones, Bill Minors, Mrs Minors, Eric Langley, Norman Parkes, -?-.

AIRCRAFT · AIRCRAFT REPAIRS
AND AIRCRAFT COMPONENTS

Helliwells Ltd

THE AIRPORT · WALSALL · STAFFS

Telephone: Walsall 4553 (6 LINES)   Telegrams: HELLIWELL Walsall

also at South Wales:
TREFOREST TRADING ESTATE
PONTYPRIDD
GLAMORGANSHIRE

London:
5, CLARGES STREET,
PICCADILLY
LONDON · W·I

New York:
BLAIR, COMINGS & HUGHES, INC
521, FIFTH AVENUE,
NEW YORK

Helliwells Ltd, who moved into a factory at Walsall Airport, became famous for their advertising after the war. With the slogan 'They who look ahead' it resembled the corporate identity advertising of recent times.

Rihgt: One of their post-war contracts was refurbishing Seafires, and Ted Roberts is seen working on one outside their factory.

Below: This is the executive aircraft fleet maintained at Walsall by Helliwells for their parent company, Tube Investments. Left to right: Rapide, Dove and Globe Swift, an American light plane for which they were agents.

An aerial view of Walsall Airport in 1947. Helliwells' factory is on the left, and the club hangars near the top.

A De Havilland Don being destroyed by small boys at the airport just before its closure in 1957.

Five

Wolverhampton Airport

Front cover of the official programme for the opening of
Wolverhampton Airport in June 1938.

The original Wolverhampton Airport buildings as they appeared in 1938, the sole hangar on the left, and terminal/clubhouse on the right.

The Midland Aero Club became the resident flying club at Pendeford, but its aircraft and operations were split with Castle Bromwich, depicted here with four of the club's five Moth Majors.

Aircraft gathered for the official opening of the airport on 25 June 1938. Left to right: Midland Aero Club's Moth Major, G-ACOG, Miles Falcon Six, G-ADLC, and Avro 626, G-ACFW.

One of the official guests at the opening, the legendary Amy Johnson, leaving the hangar.

Above: The Duke of Gloucester being introduced to Mrs Probert during his visit on 28 June 1939. He had flown to Wolverhampton to visit boys' clubs in the area. The Mayor, Councillor R.E. Probert, is next to his wife, and the Town Clerk, Mr J. Brock-Allen, is on the left.

Right: The King and Queen walking through a guard of honour formed by members of the Auxiliary Fire Service at the airport on 20 June 1940. The King and Queen also toured the Boulton Paul factory.

Opposite above: The Chief Flying Instructor, Wilfred Sutcliffe, showing the Lady Mayoress, Mrs Probert, the cabin of a Hornet Moth owned by Richard Evans.

Opposite below: The gathered dignitaries watching the flying display. Flt. Lt. A.E. Clouston (third on the right), who officially opened the airport, had just made a record-breaking flight to South Africa.

During the Second World War Wolverhampton Airport was occupied by No. 28 Elementary Flying Training School, equipped with 108 Tiger Moths. This is the 400 hr inspection team in 1945, in front of one of their charges.

Opposite above: Foster-Wickner Wicko, G-AFJB, at the airport, date unknown. In 1938 it was presented to the Midland Aero Club by the *Express* and *Star*, and named *Wulfrun II*. During the war it was used by the RAF, and post-war appeared in at least two Goodyear Trophy Air Races at Wolverhampton. The aircraft still exists in Coventry.

Opposite below: Miles Magister, G-AHNV, of the Wolverhampton Aero Club, post-war. Wolverhampton Aviation operated the airport initially after the war and were Miles service agents.

An annual feature of the airport for many years was the Goodyear Trophy Air Race, the first being held in June 1948.

Miles Aerovan, G-AJOF, at the 1949 race. It was at the airport for a short while awaiting a buyer.

The winner of the 1949 race, a Piper PA-12 Super Cruiser, flown by G. Reid-Walker, a 24 year old from Shifnal, and a Wolverhampton Aero Club member.

Goodyear's own Miles Gemini, G-AKGE, based at the airport for many years.

Part of the huge crowd gathered for the 1950 races, which included the King's Cup, the only time the country's premier air race was held at Wolverhampton. The Anson belonged to No. 28 Reserve Flying Training School which was based at Wolverhampton.

The start of the 1950 Goodyear Air Trophy. The aircraft left to right are Hawk Speed Six, G-ADGP, Gemini, G-AKKB, Falcon, G-ADFH and Wicko, G-AFJB.

The Parnall Heck 2C, G-AEGI, after repair by Wolverhampton Aviation, in March 1951. It had had its tail chopped off at the end of the previous year's King's Cup by a Spitfire VC flown by Miss R.M. Sharpe.

A Miles Gemini, believed to be one of the six assembled by Wolverhampton Aviation from parts bought after the closure of Miles Aircraft.

Above: Line-up for the start of the 1951 Goodyear Trophy Air Race. Left to right: Hawk Trainer, G-AKMN (of Ron Paine who came third), Comper Swift G-ABUS (of Tony Cole who came second) Hawk Trainer, G-AHNV. The race was won by Fred Dunkerley in the Miles M28 Mercury, G-AHAA.

Below: The first three pilots home. Left to right: Tony Cole, Fred Dunkerley and Ron Paine, in front of Tony Cole's Comper Swift.

Opposite above: The beautiful Percival Q6, G-AHOM, of Ductile Steels, which was based at Wolverhampton in the early 1950s.

Opposite below: Another corporate resident of the airport for many years, the Rapide, G-AKPA, of Midland Metal Spinning.

An unusual item in the 1952 display, which preceded the Goodyear Trophy, a Fiesler Storch of the RAE displaying its astonishing slow flying capabilities.

The Minister of Aviation, one John Profumo, arriving by BEA S-61 helicopter for the 1952 race. The aircraft in the centre, Hawk Speed Six G-ADGP, won the race in the hands of Ron Paine, Director of Air Schools Ltd, the parent company of Wolverhampton Aviation. On the right is Proctor, G-AHNA.

Alan Cambridge, a well known Aero Club member for many years, in front of a Percival Proctor.

White linen tablecloths in the airport dining-room, and two biplane airliners waiting outside. This could be anywhere in the Empire in the 1920s or '30s, but is in fact Wolverhampton Airport in the mid-1950s, Bushbury Hill being visible through the windows. At this time Wolverhampton actually had its own scheduled airline services, flown by Derby Aviation and Don Everall Aviation, to the Channel Islands and the Isle of Man, using Dragon Rapides.

Opposite above: G-AGLR, one of the Rapides used by Don Everall Aviation, which had taken over the running of the airport. Steps are in place for passengers.

Opposite below: Another of Don Everall's Rapides, G-AKZO, showing the graceful lines of this beautiful airliner.

In April 1956 the film *The Man in the Sky*, starring Jack Hawkins, was made at Pendeford. The Bristol Freighter which appeared in the film had a slight accident and ended up in a ditch. Jack Hawkins is seen here shaking hands with the pilot, Charles Helliwell.

One of the longest residents was this Chrislea Super Ace, G-AKVF. A much disliked aircraft, many newly qualified club members bought it over the years but very quickly put it up for sale! It is seen here being repaired after an in-flight instrument fire.

The largest aircraft ever to land on Pendeford's grass runways was the Bristol Beverley, during two of the air displays in the mid-1960s. This is believed to be the 1964 visit.

The last manager of the airport, and Don Everall's operation, was Eric Holden. Compare this picture with that of the callow youth on page 45.

Above and below: One of the club Tiger Moths framed by the wing and undercarriage of one of Don Everall's DC-3s. The DC-3s were operated mostly from Elmdon, but were maintained at Wolverhampton.

The airport fire crew suitably wrapped up on a snowy day.

Tiger Moth, G-AHUE, by the fuel pumps. Tiger Moths were the most familiar aircraft at Wolverhampton before, during and after the war. This will be in the late 1960s as Percival Provost, G-ASMC, is visible in the hangar.

The unfortunate end of a pupil's first cross-country solo in Tiger Moth, G-ANLP. The crash was near his parents' home near Worcester. It is amazing the number of inexperienced young men who crash near their home, or girlfriend's home.

British Aircraft Corporation's Heron, G-AREC, on a visit to Wolverhampton. Such corporate aircraft movements are one of the benefits of a municipal airport.

Actresses Sue Lawton and Noele Gordon at Pendeford to film an episode of *Crossroads* in the mid-1960s.

Above: The little two-seat Druine Turbi, G-APFA, owned by Keith Sedgewick, a long-term resident at Pendeford. In the background are two of the four wartime hangars erected at the airport. Only the one on the right was normally used for aircraft after the war.

Left: Three Stampes of the Rothman's Aerobatic Team, and Bob Mitchell's KZ-8, at the 1967 Air Display.

Opposite above: An auspicious little resident for a number of years, the single-seat Tipsy Nipper, G-APYB, in which P.G. Bannister won the King's Cup.

Below: The American midget racer Cosmic Wind, G-ARUL, in P.G. Bannister's workshop at Trysull. It had been completely rebuilt following its crash at the start of a race at Halfpenny Green in the hands of its previous owner.

The only home-built aircraft to fly at Pendeford, the Luton Minor G-ATKH. The pilot taking it out for its first flight is PFA Inspector D.G. Jones. If he looks worried it was because the engine was down 400 rpm and he only just scraped over the Marsh Lane fence. He had insufficient flying speed to bank and resorted to a very wide and flat circuit which took 15 minutes, and was a very relieved man when he finally landed.

Opposite above: Boulton Paul apprentice Peter Edgington receiving an award in front of the Don Everall Piper Colt, G-ARNI. Boulton Paul operated a subsidized flying club for their employees for many years.

Opposite below: Dave Bateman and the Taylor monoplane he built himself c. 1969. Unfortunately he stalled and crashed soon after, while flying over his home in Penn.

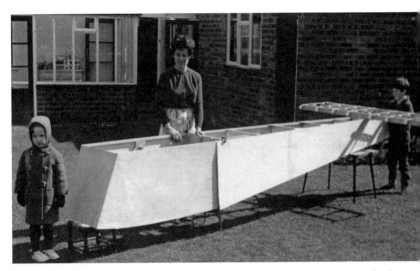

Keith Sedgewick's aircraft construction facility in Grasmere Close, Wolverhampton. The fuselage of his heavily redesigned Currie Wot is given an airing, with his family in attendance.

A while later, the fuselage now has wheels, fin and rudder, and Keith is by the nose pretending to check the wheel.

The engine is now fitted, and the fuselage is nearly finished. Keith was posing for the *Express* and *Star* in 1969.

The re-designated Super Wot, G-AVEY, in the air, being flown by Keith. It is sporting a colourful US Navy colour scheme.

Above: The last aircraft at Pendeford was this Messenger, G-AHUI, shown here after removal to the Air Scouts in Wharf Street, who had sawn off its wings.

Opposite above: Sheila Scott's Piper Comanche, G-ATOY, at Pendeford after the completion of her record-breaking round-the-world flight. It is covered with the signatures of people she met en route.

Opposite below: Sign at the airport entrance after its closure. I had permission to remove it along with the main airport sign, and I am shown undoing the screws. In the end, however, and to my eternal regret I decided to leave it in place as it was so faded.

A forlorn sight: the derelict control tower after closure in 1970, with the gutted cabin of a Piper Cherokee alongside.

Six

The Second World War

Flight Sergeant Jack Owen of Deansfield Road,
Wolverhampton, who will have to represent
the many Black Country airmen who fought
in all wars, especially those who did not
come back. Joining the RAF at the start of
the war he served two tours flying Whitley
bombers with No. 10 Sqn. at Leeming before
being transferred to No. 138 Sqn., the first
of the Moon squadrons at the secret base at
Tempsford.

Jack Owen on the left with the crew of his 10 Sqn. Whitley. He also flew Whitleys with No. 138 Sqn., dropping agents and supplies into occupied Europe. He died when his aircraft hit high ground while searching for a drop zone at low altitude over Calvados, Normandy. Only the tail gunner survived. The other four crew were buried in Vire cemetery, later being transferred to the Allied cemeteries at Caen. Owen was 21 years old.

Opposite above: A Spitfire Mk. V bought by donations from the people of Halesowen. These presentation aircraft were mostly Spitfires, the glamour aircraft of the war.

Opposite below: The first of two Walsall Spitfires, R7139, a Mk. 1. Apart from direct donations, there were also of course appeals for aluminium saucepans to be turned into Spitfires.

In the hour of peril, people of Willenhall
earned the gratitude of the British Nations
sustaining the valour of the Royal Air Force
and fortifying the cause of freedom by the
gift of Hurricane Aircraft.

"They shall mount up with wings as eagles."

Willenhall's Spitfire, AB251, a Mk. VB, though this commemorative postcard indicates that it was a Hurricane!

Spitfires awaiting conversion back to saucepans. A Mk. 22, PK717, awaiting scrap, with a row of others at RAF Cosford in the mid-1950s.

Seven

RAF Perton

The headquarters building of the wartime RAF airfield at Perton. This building, by the traffic lights on the A41, is now incorporated into a residential home. Built as a fighter base, RAF Perton only served as a satellite for the training bases at Shawbury, Tern Hill and Wheaton Aston.

LIST OF PLANS AND OTHER DOCUMENTS
REFERRED TO IN RECITAL (b) ON PAGE 1
OF BUILDING CONTRACT MADE BETWEEN
(1) THE MINISTER OF DEFENCE OF THE
KINGDOM OF THE NETHERLANDS AND
(2) BUCKS & MIDDLESEX ESTATES LIMITED
WHICH CONTRACT IS DATED THE 23rd DAY
OF October 1940.

LIST NUMBERS.	IDENT-IFICATION LETTERS.	DESCRIPTION.	NUMBER OF BUILDINGS.
1	M	LEGION HEADQUARTERS, Plan	1
2	"	" " , Sections, Elevation	1
3	J	BATT: OFFICERS' QUARTERS, Plan	6
4	"	" " " Sections, Elevation	6
5	K	OFFICERS' BATH-HOUSE, Plan	3
6	L	" MESS, Plan and Elevation	3
7	O	SOLDIERS' CANTEEN, Plan and Elevation	3
8	"	" , Section	3
9	G	CELLS TO GUARDROOMS, Plan and Elevation	3
10	Q & S	CART & CYCLE SHEDS	3
10	"	URINALS	12
11	R	CAR MAINTENANCE SHOP, Complete Plan	3
12	D	SOLDIERS' BATH-HOUSE, " "	18
13	T1	PRISON, Plan	1
14	T2	" , Elevation, Sections	1
15	LAING	LAING PORTABLE HUT, Complete plan	126
16	A	SOLDIERS' QUARTERS, Plan	60
16	B	COY. COMMANDER'S OFFICE, Plan	15
16	C	STORE HUT, Plan	33
16	E	N.C.O.'S QUARTERS, Plan	3
16	F	BATT. COMMANDER'S OFFICE, Plan	3
16	I	MAINTENANCE HUT, Plan	3
17	H	DOCTOR'S CONSULTING ROOM, Plan	3
17	P	N.C.O.'S MESS, Plan	3
17	G1	GUARDROOM, Plan	3
18	LIST	HEATING STOVES	
19	SPEC.	DETAIL OF HEATING & EQUIPMENT	
20	LIST	ELECTRIC EQUIPMENT	
21	SPEC.	DETAIL OF ELECTRIC EQUIPMENT	
22	LIST	SANITARY EQUIPMENT	
23	SPEC.	DETAIL OF SANITARY EQUIPMENT	

NOTE. Although this List comprises details and particulars of all
the main buildings, it is not to be taken as completely comprehensive.
There remain a number of subsidiary buildings and works still to be
designed and projected, such as boiler houses, electricity sub-
stations, pumping stations, sewage works, etc. The layout plans
of the Camp are now being projected on the site, and these will be
treated as incorporated in the Contract, together with plans and
specifications of roads, drains, electrical and water mains, as
soon as they are ready. Any works of any kind needed in connection
with the construction and proper execution of this Camp shall be
deemed to form part of the Contract, notwithstanding the fact that
they may not form part of the present List.

FOR IDENTIFICATION of this List the Signatures of the parties have
been affixed hereto and to the Plans and other Documents herein
specified this 23rd day of October 1940.

.... ALBERTUS QUIRINUS HENDRIKUS DIJXHOORN
Minister of Defence of the Kingdom of the Netherlands.

.... HENRY WYNMALEN, Managing Director of
Bucks & Middlesex Estates Limited.

The contract turning the residential buildings at Perton over to the Dutch Army, to be occupied by the Princess Irene Brigade.

Dutch soldiers helping to build their own camp. Many ties were made between the Dutch and the local people during the war.

The large garage building under construction. Many extra buildings were erected for the Dutch.

RAF Perton was also used by Boulton Paul Aircraft and Helliwells to test Douglas Bostons, for which they had modification contracts. This one, BZ435, is having equipment removed before flying to Pendeford.

This is a view of the equipment under the upper hatch of BZ435, shown open in the upper photograph.

Eight

Boulton Paul Aircraft Ltd

Boulton & Paul Ltd began building aircraft at Norwich in 1915. In 1934 their aircraft department was sold off to become Boulton Paul Aircraft Ltd, and moved to a brand new factory at Pendeford in 1936. This is K8310, the prototype of their most famous product, the Defiant fighter, the first of the 1,062 which they eventually built.

The new Boulton Paul factory under construction in 1936.

The first aircraft built at Pendeford was the Hawker Demon two-seat fighter. This shows several of the 106 built awaiting delivery in 1937.

Lord Gorell, Chairman of Boulton Paul Aircraft, cutting the first sod for the new extension to the factory on 19 May 1937. Alongside, left to right, are Herbert Strictland (Joint Managing Director), J.L. Wood (Secretary), Air Cdr. A.G. Gill, W.S. Hatrell (Architect), -?-, -?-, -?-, -?-, H.J. Whittick (Editor, *Express* and *Star*), Alderman A. Baldwin Bantock, Councillor Kidson, J.D. North (Joint Managing Director and Chief Engineer), Viscount Sandon (Director), and Sir Charles Mander (Mayor).

The Defiant prototype showing sleek lines before the turret was fitted, ready for its first flight on 11 August 1937.

Following the Demon onto the production lines was the Blackburn Roc, all 136 being built by Boulton Paul.

A production Roc, which was basically a Skua fitted with a Boulton Paul Type A four-gun turret, all detail design work being carried out by Boulton Paul.

Robin Lindsay Neale (centre) about to test fly a Roc. He was assistant to Chief Test Pilot Cecil Feather, and later became Chief Test Pilot himself on Feather's retirement.

The Defiant prototype, K8310, now with the turret fitted. In the flight shed behind can just be seen an Overstrand turret on a stand, removed from Overstrand K8176, and replaced by the first Defiant turret for testing.

A Lockheed Hudson, N7251, at Pendeford in March 1940. The Hudson was a militarized Lockheed 14 airliner with a Boulton Paul Type C, two-gun turret in the dorsal position. On the Halifax heavy bomber the Type C was also fitted in the nose position.

Production Defiants awaiting delivery in July 1940. The Air Ministry-supplied Bellman hangars on the left and the main factory have now been camouflaged.

The Boulton Paul Type E four-gun tail turret, as fitted to the Halifax and RAF Liberators. The Type E together with the Type A (dorsal) and Type C (nose/dorsal) turrets were the main production turrets of the war.

'Paradise Airport', the dummy Boulton Paul factory built a mile along the Shropshire Union Canal from the real thing, complete with dummy aircraft on the dummy airfield. The imitation bus-turning circle has been left thoroughly conspicuous, presumably to draw German bombers. It did not work; the sole bombing raid targeted the real thing.

Opposite above: Aerial view of the camouflaged factory with aircraft outside the flight sheds on the right.

Opposite below: The Boulton Paul Home Guard unit ready to defend factory and airfield against all-comers.

A view of Pendeford Airfield from the north. Boulton Paul is at the bottom, the new buildings of the airfield are being built on the upper left, and the airfield itself has been disguised with painted 'hedgerows'. Almost dead centre are five blast pens cut into the hillside, each designed to hold two aircraft.

Opposite above: The Defiant prototype, K8310, in August 1940, with the turret removed once more, as a proposed single-seat fighter with forward-firing guns.

Opposite below: Three Boulton Paul test pilots in front of a Defiant night fighter. Left to right: Colin Evans (who died test flying a Fairey Firefly), Chief Test Pilot Cecil Feather and Robin Lindsay Neale (who lost his life in a Balliol crash after the War).

Many women workers were employed in the factory during the war. These are making the retractable wooden fairings fitted either side of the Defiant's turret.

As a contrast this is a posed publicity shot using a model. She is depicted in other photographs undertaking many different tasks wearing a pristine white coat and stiletto heels!

The second prototype Mark II Defiant, with a more powerful Merlin engine. Posed groundshots of the Defiant invariably show the turret pointing forward, the one direction the guns could not fire.

Aircrew of No. 264 Sqn., the first Defiant unit, being given a silver salver to commemorate shooting down their first hundred German aircraft. (At the time it is said they had actually only managed ninety-eight!)

The P92/2, a half-scale flying model of the proposed four-cannon turret fighter, the P92. This was ordered as a Defiant replacement, but cancelled when only 5 per cent complete.

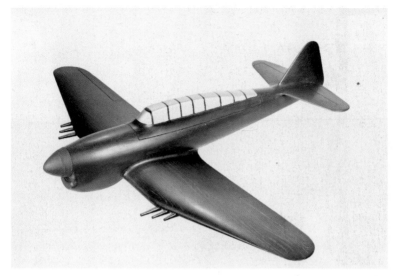

A model of another potential Defiant replacement, the two-seat P96. In this form it has Sabre engine, and six forward firing cannon. It was also available with a turret and different engines, but was never ordered.

Sir Stafford Cripps talking to a woman engaged on turret cupola assembly, and clearly asking for the name of her hairdresser.

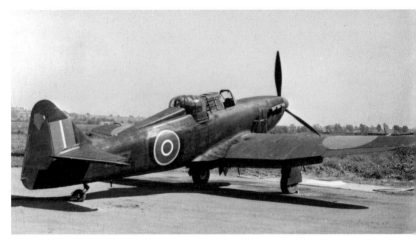

A Defiant night fighter equipped with radar. The Defiant was the most successful night fighter of the Blitz.

A Halifax, R9436, experimentally equipped with the Boulton Paul Type T turret with twin 0.5-in machine-guns. Disgracefully Boulton Paul were not allowed to put heavy weapon turrets into production until the last months of the war.

A display in the Civic Hall, Wolverhampton, showing Boulton Paul's contribution to the war effort.

A Defiant target tug at Pendeford. Target tug versions were built new and also converted from fighters which were surplus to requirements.

The Fairey Barracuda followed the Defiant on to the production lines, and 692 were built. This is one of a remarkable series of photographs following the production of one every few days from fuselage frame to complete aircraft. This is dated 10 July 1942.

The aircraft has now progressed to final assembly, and the date is 4 September 1942.

The completed aircraft is wheeled from the factory on its production trolley. Wings were then unfolded, wheels lowered, and it was test flown. This photograph is not part of the series, but shows DP860 on 8 April 1943.

This was Boulton Paul's offering for a Barracuda replacement, the P105. It was offered with different engines, and in different configurations for different roles. This is the recce version with ventral glazing for the observer. It was never ordered.

After the war Boulton Paul refurbished 270 Wellington bombers and converted them to T10 navigation trainers. This one, NC894, had an argument with the Marsh Lane railings.

Opposite above: The wing of Hawker Sea Fury, VB857, the first of an order for one hundred cancelled at the end of the war. The nearly completed aircraft was taken to Hawker's at Langley to be finished, and served as one of two Sea Fury prototypes.

Opposite below: This Airspeed Oxford was purchased after the war as a company aircraft, and was a feature of Pendeford Airport until the 1960s. It is now in the museum at Duxford.

Most wartime turret production was undertaken by Joseph Lucas. After the war one of the Bellman hangars at Pendeford was converted to turret production, and here Lincoln Type F nose turrets are being made.

The prototype Balliol T1 advanced trainer, VL892, with Courtaulds' chimneys in the background. It was flown initially with this Bristol Mercury engine, because the Mamba turbo-prop was not yet ready.

The drawing office in July 1948. This woodblock floor is now empty, and the drawing office is nearer reception, with computers at every desk and hardly a drawing table in sight.

The second prototype Balliol T1, VL917, the first aircraft in the world to be powered by a single turbo-prop, an Armstrong-Siddeley Mamba.

The Boulton Paul apprentices in December 1948. Back row, left to right: first four unknown, ? Haycocks, next four unknown, Alan Green, John Taff, Brian Castley, George Richards, next two unknown, Peter Stone, Reg Green, Archie Onions, Phil Harris. Third row: Alan Butler, Clive Birchall, Dave Young, ? Fellows, unknown, Tony Southwood, unknown, ? Goodman, next two unknown, Brian Holmes, rest unknown. Second row: Roy Conway, George Rous, Ray Anthony, Lewis Chesney, unknown, Horace Jones, ? Reynolds, ? Ford, Tom Flavell, Ken Slaney, Brian Tovell, Peter Taylor. Front row: all unknown except Alan Hughes, far right.

The Gust Alleviation Lancaster, fitted by Boulton Paul with a probe for detecting gusts, which then caused automatic corrective action with the ailerons.

A model of the P113 project in the wind tunnel. This was to be an experimental supersonic aircraft in which the pilot sat in a semi-prone position inside the intake.

This unusual picture is taken on the taxiway to the airfield inside a P113 model nose, to show the visibility the pilot would have.

Pre-production Balliol T2s in the flight shed. It had been decided that production Balliols would be powered by the Merlin piston engine.

The wreckage of the prototype Balliol T2 in a field near Coven. The windscreen had disintegrated during a power dive and Chief Test Pilot Robin Lindsay Neale and his assistant Peter Tishaw died.

Opposite above: The first Balliol T2 for the Royal Ceylon Air Force, CA301, before crating for dispatch. A total of twelve were exported.

Opposite below: New Chief Test Pilot A.E. 'Ben' Gunn (right), and his assistant Richard 'Dickie' Mancus (left) with naval officers in front of Sea Balliol T21, WL721, one of thirty built for the Fleet Air Arm.

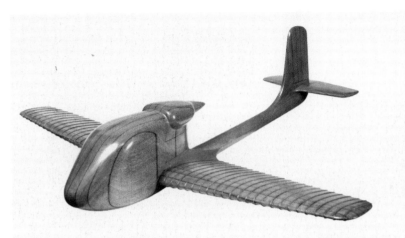

A model of the P110 project, an unusual design for a three-seat light aircraft produced in the immediate post-war years.

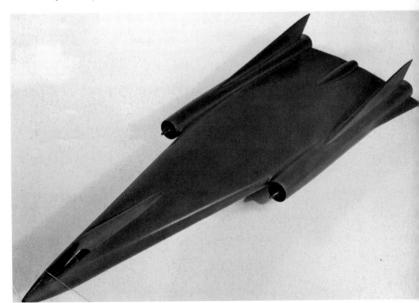

A very different project indeed. This was the P133 supersonic VTOL strike aircraft offered in 1956, with twin Gyron Junior engines and fan lift.

'The Brain', one of the earliest computers, developed at Boulton Paul in the early 1950s. I imagine its capacity would be equalled today by something the size of a credit card.

A full-size mock-up of the P119 applied jet trainer in October 1950. The company had high hopes for this design but there was little official interest.

Ben Gunn doing what all fighter pilots do with their hands, watched by visiting pilots from the Empire Test Pilots School, with the P119 mock-up behind.

A Sea Balliol suffering an undercarriage collapse on HMS *Triumph*.

An aerial view of the factory in 1950, with two Wellingtons just visible by the Bellman hangars.

One of the few jets to fly from Pendeford's grass runways, this is a Nene-powered Vampire, which had been fitted with new intakes and tail by Boulton Paul Aircraft.

The P111 delta-wing research aircraft about to undertake taxiing trials at Pendeford, still unpainted.

The P111's anti-spin parachute being deployed as a braking chute, probably the only time this has been seen at Pendeford.

Ben Gunn in front of a Canberra at Defford. For fourteen years Boulton Paul Aircraft were the main contractors for most Canberra modifications.

Powered flying controls were becoming the company's staple during the 1950s. This unit is from a Valiant bomber.

The P124 jet trainer designed to meet the same requirements as the Jet Provost, which was of course preferred.

The last production Balliol on the apron, with Dickie Mancus, fifth from left, about to fly it.

The Boulton Paul apprentice picture of 1959. The Balliol behind is the company's own demonstrator, G-ANSF. It had been grounded for three years at the time, and was largely only used for the annual apprentice pictures before being broken up, by the apprentices.

Boulton Paul's last design to fly, the P120 delta-wing research aircraft, VT951.

The P120 in the air, newly painted all-black, for the Farnborough Show of 1952. After eleven hours of flying it crashed, following elevon failure, and Ben Gunn became the first pilot to eject from a delta-wing aircraft.

A Royal Aeronautical Society lecture in the canteen in 1961, given by Chief Designer Fred Crocombe (standing, right), designer of the Blackburn Beverley before moving to Boulton Paul.

A production line of Canberra B8 noses in 1961, with the Balliol, G-ANSF, and the modified Balliol to the right, awaiting their final fate.

Above: A visit of French officials by Avro 748 in connection with Concorde, for which Dowty Boulton Paul supplied the powered flying control units. J.D. North (second left) is greeting the French Minister of Aviation, with the British Minister of Aviation Roy Jenkins alongside.

Opposite below: The Balliol production line re-opened. Two Balliol front fuselages under restoration by the Boulton Paul Association in the factory where one of them, WN149, was first made. The other, WN534, was one of thirty Balliols made by Blackburn

Right: Jack Holmes working in the rear fuselage of a pre-production Balliol, 2BA spanner in hand, in 1950. His father had joined Boulton & Paul in Norwich in the 1920s, and was one of the many Norfolk men who came to Wolverhampton with the company. Both his sons, Jack and Brian, became BPA apprentices.

Below: Same man, same aircraft, same 2BA spanner, forty years later! Jack Holmes working on the restoration of Balliol WN149 in 1993, showing that a good workman looks after his tools!

Sir Charles Mander (left) bidding farewell to J.D. North after a visit to Boulton Paul. John Dudley North was the greatest unsung British aircraft pioneer. He was Chief Engineer of the Grahame-White Company at Hendon in 1913, when only 21 years old, and from 1915 until his death in 1968 was the guiding light of Boulton Paul Aircraft.

Acknowledgements

Photographs for this book have come from a variety of sources, the largest number being from the archives of Dowty Boulton Paul Ltd, mostly of Boulton Paul Aircraft, but also of RAF Perton and Pendeford Airport.

I drew on the collection of Group Captain Edwin Shipley for many of the Walsall photographs, some of which were taken from his books *A Short History of Walsall Aviation* and *The Green Eagles of Calshot*. Other Walsall photographs and many of Wolverhampton Airport came from the collection of the late Eric Holden.

I once more borrowed photographs from Jim Boulton, mainly of Dunstall Park, and Jack Chambers, of Wolverhampton Airport; and further large collections of Wolverhampton photographs came from Keith Sedgwick, and N.D. Welch.

The pictures of Dolly Shepherd came from the book *When the 'Chute Went up* by Dolly Shepherd, with the kind permission of her daughter Molly Sedgewick, who gives lectures on the exploits of her mother.

Further photographs came from Wolverhampton Central Library, Walsall Local Studies Centre, Cannock Library, the Boulton Paul Association, the Princess Irene Brigade Museum, and the RAF Museum.

Individuals who helped with the book or who lent photographs were Michael Dancer, John Godwin, Jack Holmes, P.R. Johnson, Arthur Lloyd, Maurice Marsh, Fred Mason, Fred Owen, and not least Wendy Matthiason.

I have to thank all these organizations and individuals for their kind help, and to anyone I have missed, I apologize.